Blood, Sparrows and Sparrows

Blood, Sparrows and Sparrows

Eugenia Leigh

FOUR WAY BOOKS
TRIBECA

Please direct all inquiries to:
Editorial Office
Four Way Books
POB 535, Village Station
New York, NY 10014
www.fourwaybooks.com

Library of Congress Cataloging-in-Publication Data

Leigh, Eugenia.
Blood, sparrows and sparrows / Eugenia Leigh.
pages cm
ISBN 978-1-935536-49-9 (pbk. : alk. paper)
I. Title.
PS3612.E35655B58 2014
811'.6--dc23
2014011321

This book is manufactured in the United States of America and printed on acid-free paper.

Four Way Books is a not-for-profit literary press. We are grateful for the assistance we receive from individual donors, public arts agencies, and private foundations.

This publication is made possible with public funds from the National Endowment for the Arts

and from the New York State Council on the Arts, a state agency

and from the Jerome Foundation.

We are a proud member of the Council of Literary Magazines and Presses.

Distributed by University Press of New England
One Court Street, Lebanon, NH 03766

CONTENTS

I. BLOOD

II. BLOOD

III. BLOOD

IV. SPARROWS

FOR MY SISTERS

You are worth hundreds of sparrows.

I. BLOOD

She stepped over her creator,
spreading his blood across the polished floor,
and then walked out of the factory and into the storm.

— SALVADOR PLASCENCIA, *THE PEOPLE OF PAPER*

The Morning I Abandoned My Father, Angels

materialized everywhere—
not a flock, not a crowd. They hovered
like dust. Like flames

choking his home or suns plunging
from his roof, his veins. The flames, the suns
thrashing. The good wings

of good beasts. And my mother's voice,
flapping in my blood: *If you need to run, run.*
But if you regret this, do not *blame me.*

The Deposition

All I recall from 1991:   a stairwell
sprouts from a cafeteria to a playground. Jesus sits
at the bend. As blobs of children rumble ahead, I turn
to ask if he'd like company. *I'm alright*, Jesus says. *Go have fun.*

What does it mean that I remember dreams and not real life?

I was born   with a black hole in my brain. The first time
I noticed the hole,   I was twelve. In the back office
of a glorified daycare, I said   nothing
until the skittish social worker admitted, *Yes,*

that's a two-way mirror, and behind it, a thousand
suits are whittling your words to knife
your father's spine in court.   Later that day, my mother
shook me—   screaming—*Why did you lie?*

Why didn't you tell her he beat you across the head?

I stared at her.   Who did what?   Black hole.

*

Last night, the oncologist reduced Grandpa's morphine drip
to let my sister tilt the phone to a lucid ear.
Five hundred miles   away, I rehearsed
my breaths.   I pictured   his sunken chest,

plastic tubes linking his lungs to my grandmother's
prayers.   When did I last see him?   I remember
Grandpa everywhere. Feeding us.   But sometimes
I remember him   not at all. Not even his face.

Within the hour, my sister called back to say
he died.   *But first, he opened his eyes.*

*

My still life childhood   crumbles like a photograph
brittle   in the fists of an arsonist.

We get one thousand words per burning photograph,
yet this is all I've got: my mother's kneeling
shrieks.   My father's voice full of boils.   My sisters'
flinching, my wincing, and now,   cracking

at the edge of my frigid Brooklyn rooftop, I hear

all of us   blaring from that black hole.

Recognizing Lightning

When the school tornado alert
shriveled my little sister
hysterical in her snail position,
I marched to her third grade classroom
and thought, *This is it.*
Time to be brave. Thought the same
at age six, home alone
with both baby sisters, one hand
toweling my scalp spewing blood,
the other holding
the phone, calming our mother.
And here we were—
my sister and I—two adults
trekking thousands of miles east
and me, begging to switch seats.
Kansas torrents smeared
the highway blank. I steered
according to the GPS screen, aiming
my car, clogged with all our belongings,
for the neon green pixels.
If my sister hadn't mentioned
          Dorothy and her twister,
     I wouldn't have started bawling.
                    You drive through the storm.
          Please—
We switched seats.
                    My sister drove
and I phoned B, who made up
something about the Greeks

recognizing lightning as the source
of negative ions. Fertile soil
for art.
You're lucky, he said.
Write this down.

Pretty Universe

God stalked me on Marion Avenue. Said, *You can't*
fix it. Then, *I can't either.*   That morning,

my ceiling lamp had ripped from its cord. Even after
I welded the fragments with duct tape, everything
felt cracked—like your five-hundred dollar glasses

I smashed that winter—so I thought, if I couldn't fix that,
what the hell am I doing piecing together
your eyes? Our crumbling

kisses? So I didn't question God. Sometimes, God wants
to be understood. Sometimes, God hates

his perfect grammar. His pretty
universe. So he'll pluck a butterfly of its left wing. Call it
art. He'll turn from a hurricane. Say, *It wasn't me.*

If artists were created in his image, how often
does God abandon *his* mistakes?

The day I stopped talking to you, I said
nothing to him too. I cursed. My entire drive home.
I littered the freeway with fistfuls of tissues

while God shuffled his God feet
and pretended not to see.

The Unraveling

In a California no one will ever see again,
My father is beginning to die.
— Larry Levis, "Winter Stars"

Windows down on I-70, I hoard the oxygen
stored in Ohio. I know when I reach home,
Joshua trees won't scratch clean

my lungs of ash and recession.
Once I wheel past the Midwest,
California gapes at me with the pitted frame

of a parched beggar. She bends
shamefully away from the Pacific. Lies as stiff
as a terminal patient who refuses prayer

not because God isn't real, but because God is
too real. It's become easier to want to die
than to want to live forever.

Immigrants wilt in California's shadow. My mother
among them. Where I once suckled
the nipples of citrus fruits, the land slouches

pockmarked with abandon—thirty-seven million
pairs of hands folded into themselves, one hand
occasionally opening to throw a coin into a cup.

A man rests on the bottom step
of a church. A depleted waitress feeds Sacramento
and wraps the leftovers for her children.

The sun creeps behind a screen
of unfamiliar clouds. I return to work—
what else can I do? A preacher finds the man on the step

and offers his flask—what else can he do?
The man declines and pores over a photograph
of a kiss. He says, quietly, *Some weather we're having.*

Half Glance

The ex locates my new home and sends a photo
of his fingerprints. A ghost of nicotine in the folds

of the envelope. No caption. No note. Only ten
wrinkled, mouthless orphans exposed on a bed
of paper, one edge plucked awry from its spiral bind.

The next day, a photo of the crease in his stockbroker
slacks, dollar-flat. And here, a blurry photo
of the alarm clock I bought him as a thank you

for the alarm clock he bought me. A photo of arbitrary
minutes—7:10, hollow, starved of sentiment
like a picture of a planet blundered together by molecular

collision—a photo snapped by God,

who gave the cosmic accident a half glance and thought,
This might hang nicely on my wall.

On the Anniversary of the War on Terror

A husband tears off his wife's legs and pins them to a wall
next to a painting of peeled bananas. Men
journey from all over the world to admire those legs.
For a fee, the husband gives an esteemed journalist
permission to bite a thigh. The journalist begs to bag
a slice to show his unruly wife (and the neighbors
who malign this unruly wife). The husband allows the slice.
Weeks later, when the kicking begins, the husband
shuts down the exhibit after his wife's left foot
makes excellent contact with the President's skull.
That evening, the news reports an emergency bill
passed by the President. He demands immediate action
in support of men violently terrorized by women.

Monsters

The first time I imagined harming a man,
I was twelve. I imagined that cop
quivering in my fists.

He'd paraded my sister and me
like two prized rats. Bragged, *We rescued them*
from their kidnapper, and my mouth
sutured shut. I uncapped a permanent marker. Scrawled
onto my arms, *Please help. Monsters have stolen my dad.*

When our dad ran from California—first on foot,
then by bus—did he drag us out?
Or did my sister and I chase him? He disguised us
as boys. We left our mom
messages from payphones. Survived on fries.
And the morning he was arrested
outside that Wisconsin hotel, I stitched into my eyelids

that image of him clinched in handcuffs, mouthing
assurance from the back of that howling car.

                        Nine years later, at Incheon International Airport,
        I don't recognize him, cloaked in monstrous welts.
How does he know to run to me,
older than Mom was when I was born?

I had pretended it was a bus trip across the country—
our first family vacation. How could I know
my dad flushed my hair down that hotel toilet
because every cop—everywhere—was studying my photo?

When he'd joked about changing our names, my sister cried.
                    Did she believe that word?   *Kidnapper?*

I should have said, I *asked* my dad to take me.
I should have said, I promised him
I could be a boy for as long as he needed.

The Jar Party

They gravitate to my scars. Awkward
humans gasping, *Yours matches mine—*
then with biblical celebrity, cult camaraderie,
Your mom was almost   *My mom also*

We gush and hug, exchange numbers
to arrange for our mothers to meet—as though
women gather for this sort of thing—
to crochet scars over cocktails.

I collect fractured humans and store them
in a bell jar for moments

I want *normal.* Sometimes,

I shrink myself to join the jar party.
We behave like nine thousand blind people
in a room with no door—every one of us
shouting   for an exit.

II. BLOOD

There is nothing so secular that it cannot be sacred,
and that is one of the deepest messages of the Incarnation.

— Madeleine L'Engle, *Walking on Water*

Genesis

How carelessly God hummed us whole
with such pronounced
holes   for lungs.

How hollow   we are. How

anonymous—six billion
pitchers—flicked—discarded
in a faraway warehouse.

Wire Hangers

When you hold me, will you hold only my cocoa-buttered
skin or will you hold my mother's callous feet,
her cigarette-stained apron? Will you hold
my grandfather's charcoal lungs?
His beer cans? When you hold me, will you hold
my mother's rough hand, raking
nickels, food stamps from an unzipped wallet?
Will you hold her morning prayers,
her drum roll of tongues?
And when you hold me, will you hold only the stars
inked to my ankle, or will you
hold my sister's skinny arm
when I beat it out of its socket?

Will you hold the wire hangers
in my father's hand?
And when you hold those wire hangers,
the wooden ones,
the yardsticks,
will you hold my mother
down as my father whips her with them?

Will you hold the small boy version
of my father and hide him
in the trash can? Will you hold *his* father
back and put his knife
down? And when you put my grandfather's knife
down, will you pull my *father's* knife
from my pregnant mother's chest? Will you hold her
until she sings again? Will you hold
their third miracle
daughter when she is born with her infant roar,
both knees? And when you hold me, will you hold
only the lies I told our pastor
or will you hold the police report that tells
I hit the bathtub when he knocked me out?

And when the police knock
and when the police knock
again, and when the police knock
year after year after day afternoon—when the police knock
that afternoon, will you hold our apartment door open
and will you make me tell my father
I forgive him
because no one will hold him
until I do, nine years older, wired
with my own beer cans,
my hanging tongues.

Not a Warning, Not a Challenge, Not an Instruction Manual

I once slept with an older man who eclipsed
every sliver of light in his apartment with blankets,

duct tape, and ancient maps of New York.
He flinched awake every hour

on his mattress on the floor
because his childhood stalked him with a knife

at the other end of his eyelids. I orgasmed
to knowing how to make him feel better.

This was the man I used
to cheat on the lover whose parents blew out
birthday candles over a webcam.

While they ate cake in the computer screen,
I reached under my bell jar and pulled out
my mom. Pulled out her chain-smoking boyfriend.

I pulled out my alcoholic friends, all the rutty
strangers with *fail*
engraved on their necks. And I sat—

cross-legged—in a field of their wild limbs,

which no one could ever climb past.

Contrition with Liquor

Bad nights were my arms
smashing into you—gavels

to a fishbowl. Flinging
glasses at your head meant

another Wednesday. We tumbled
through months of this. Me,

passed around like a wet
sacrament. You, bridled

like a good altar boy.
You'd unleash Sunset Strip

from my liver. Flush my mouth
in sinks of cold light.

You taught me how to spit, so I spit
enough nails to fix you

right on top of Jesus.
I was too slurred to see

you were too human to unhang
yourself—and Jesus,

too crippled beneath you to help.

Deciding Not to Drown Today

A man teeters at the edge

of the East River. Is his beer half empty or half
dangerous? Buildings belch from the other side

of the river, squished inch-thin if I squint
hard enough. After his last deliberate swig, the man

lifts his bottle over his head as if considering
whether to sacrifice it. He hesitates.

He walks off, brandishing the bottle
like a trophy. Like something he almost lost.

Where is the memo about knowing
what to save, what to abort?

I drift toward the man's abandoned mark.
River murk and reflection

divine nothing.
A woman clips a leash to a toddler, and I notice

a sign asking not to climb the rocks please.
Everyone warns us off the rocks.

What will keep us from the river?

The Untold Version

I tell everyone the rapids dumped me into the Nile,
    but in the video, I appear to let go
        of the raft, the oar. I dive into the river.

In the dream, I unbuckle the life vest. Scrape off
    the helmet. I don't hold my breath—
        I gulp. In the nightmare, the Nile becomes

the stream kicking down your cheeks.
    In your delusion, I am the woman who controls
        the dam. I take a hammer to the metal. Hack

everything loose. You believe I'm both
    the villain and the damsel. In my story, you are
        scenery. You serve as backdrop

to each character climbing into my blouse. No—
    you are the stain on that blouse.
        You weren't the one

yelling *swim* in real life. In real life, I opened
    my eyes underwater. Stretched
        for light. I pictured you holding me down.

I pictured me drowning by choking on you.

Sex and Horseradish

My mother left my father more than once. A favorite
family tradition observed when I was four.
Ten. Eleven. Twelve. Leaving is easier

the second time. Like sex. Distance is an acquired
taste. Horseradish. When I first touched
a boy, I lusted for that stench

of begging. I would trap the boy in his car. Demand
he drive to the airport and park. He would reach
between my jeans. I would cry. Beg.

For no reason. Then he'd also beg and I'd let him
drive back to his large house. Let him
see his married parents again.

I left that boy. Then left the next one. Then left the next
and the next and when one tried to leave *me*, I tied
that one to my neck. He stayed for years

until I left him, too. *Flew* away,
really—his body, hanging
from my body.

Departure

The moon sags like a low bulb
in the fog. Its glow ricochets against

freeway flares—emergency pink,
the orange of my urge to cram my hands

down your old coat pockets so the holes will pull
me through your skin, past your ribs, onto a cushion

of lung. I could fondle an artery. Sink
my ankles in your bloodstream. My fingers scratch

alphabets into your scalp, rake the curls
above your nape. Los Angeles,

witless with its arrogant lights, smacks the sky dull.
Two stars refuse to dim. They watch you try

to wipe distance from my eyes. They watch me
fidget. You fragment.

The Burning Ones

The seraphim hovering over the city
thunder *holy holy holy.*
They moan and moan

that lone word—a prayer
strangled in their sober throats. We hoist
umbrellas to joust their sobs

flushing from above like crushed stars.
We ignore that gold chord
droning

and droning. We know nothing
of glory. The sky, to the polluted eye,
black as asphalt.

A toy lemur, crooked stripes. Its dog tag:
Beware of real live tiger and teeth.

*

A real live tiger and teeth
studying a human who bends into its face
to read the dog tag, which says,
Yes, really.

*

Your father—with tidier eyes,
                                        fuller facial hair.

*

A wall sprinkled with buttons.
            And your mother's phone voice—
            laughing—
                        each time you press a button.

*

Not your father at all. Instead, the busboy
who sneaks you extra gin
and winks.

*

You. Your fading freckle,
your misprinted birth certificate.
            You, pressed to a stranger
            and invisible. You, pressed to a stranger
                        and wet.

*

The stranger's weak bed.
                        Your holy insomnia.

*

Not you. Instead, the slight
buzz of arm hairs after a gift
of *I love you*—
            and all the inadequate years
                        before the next one.

*

The next one.

Aftertaste

A miniature of the man I once loved
sits in my mouth

with mounds of miniature paper. A pen. His good fists.
When I sleep, he nestles in the membrane

of my cheeks. And weeps. Rereads
a thousand pages of our smudged apologies.

When I kiss other men, he ducks
into a hole in my molar. Sometimes, he lunges
at their tongues and *every* time, his fists

unclench. He caresses the tongues instead. Holds them
and weeps some more.

One day, the miniature man pulls
my lips shut. He weighs down my tongue

with reams of paper and strings all thousand apologies
along my teeth. I waste years flossing, spitting his sorry

fragments. And him: rewriting, rewriting—

III. BLOOD

Why did god create a dual universe?
So he might say,
"Be not like me. I am alone."
And it might be heard.

— Mark Z. Danielewski, *House of Leaves*

6,883 Miles from New York, My Father Is Alive

But a man who knows the eyes
of the delivery boy better than the eyes of his daughter
is not alive. A man once caged, now
cracked, chapped with pleading
forgiveness from the living
too haunted to visit
his grave—

a man once caged, then deported—picked off from his home,
picked off like lint—cannot be alive.

It broke me to receive envelope after envelope from the dead.

It broke him never to be sure
his envelopes delivered. It breaks a girl
to repress. To shred with her unsent letters.

It breaks her to wake each day to a thicker
haunting—the dead crying with desertion.

How we dare hate
the dead! How we cripple at having been
left. But how much more—*how much more*

crippling to know *you* are the one
who left—
who left him for dead?

Upon Living with a Man Newly Released

A friend watches me spoon a soggy chunk
of my childhood and fling it
somewhere between my Brooklyn sink
and California. Her thoughts brake, as if to judge
the remains of a six-car pileup, or the sink,
jammed with crayon drawings of my father
in jail. Father, unconscious on bedding of stationery

marked with my name. Father, stick figure
twisted, and red. Father, fingering baloney
greased with the spit of a guard. Father's mouth,
gorged with sores. Father's music,
stripped from his lungs. Father's eyes,
swollen with apology to my mother,

whose Garden Grove apartment reeks
of apathy. Her boyfriend's roses. I sew together
syllables about trauma—a poem
about what war gifts to its witness
(silence). My words gurgle with curdled

blood, my mother's old bruises.
My friend, who pops therapy like candy,
hounds me to see someone. But how could I
wreck another human being with the shrieks

of my father's wars? Sometimes,
when the night is blank, I beat the new
moon with my crumpled drawings. She collects

my abuse in her belly. Waxes
until she, pregnant with rotten paper,

empties my anguish into the sky—

Impossible Questions

I want to know

what my mother stuffed into her purse
the night she left our father
and forgot to take us.

Whether she left her hymnbook
and took a comb. Whether she packed a sandwich and took
the time to spread mustard on both slices of bread.

When my mother returned the next day—all shaking bones,
heavy hair—young and gorgeous as ever with Jesus
freshly resurrected on her breath—I first kissed her.

Then kicked her.

This Malfunctioning Wing

While the man sprayed antifreeze to de-ice one wing,
the other wing froze over. I unbuckled.

I watched the man steer his cherry picker to the other wing.
Then the first wing froze over. After the fifth intercom

apology, the attendants served cold cinnamon rolls
while we sat, for ten hours, stuck too far from the airport

to walk back in the blizzard. Once we taxied to the gate,
I phoned a man I had pretended not to love

even after his skull fractured and his brain sponged
enough blood to mop over his motor skills. Neurologists said

he should have died. Maybe he'd taken enough bats
and bottles to the body for God to hand him a consolation

miracle. Packed in ice chips, ears bleeding, he whispered.
His first attempt with a telephone after his—

what did he call it? Fight? Accident? Triumph.
I abandoned him the following July to fall in love

with a man who had never broken a bone, but almost died,
in combat gear, jumping from an army aircraft. We made love

while I fingered two childhood scars embossed in his back
from reaching beneath the jagged bottoms of fence slats

to save a dying bird.
                         My mouth has endured two kinds of men:

the men who save and the men who are dying birds. I am
neither savior, nor prey, but a plane. The one they jump from.

The one that almost kills. The one they can't board
post-accident because their brains rattle. The one that carries

unforgiving people, pressing buttons, asking for ginger ale.
The one that waits, frozen, for a man to de-ice

this malfunctioning wing, then the other. The one that wants
to scourge the runway. To fly. But instead, wheels

back to where she came from. Lets all her passengers go.

The Exchange

I want an interruption.
God stirs the Pacific with a swizzle stick.
I want constellations.
God hunts for packaging tape.
Ninety-nine thunderbolts say, *Here we are*, and God hunts the wayward bolt.
God hunts a not-so-wayward cab driver, a new ghostwriter, the bitter daughters.
I offer God a map.
I offer God one chapter.
I offer God 1997.
I offer God the better pen, and God writes this note:

> *I know a man who bought a dog and named him*
> *Father.*
> *I know a girl who says Daddy*
> *when she prays.*

Blood, Sparrows and Sparrows

He said to her, "Daughter, your faith has healed you.
Go in peace and be freed from your suffering."
— Gospel of Mark, chapter 5, verse 34

Genesis, Exodus, Leviticus—a girl stitches
all sixty-six books into her wrists. Digs
flesh trenches until bloody rivers

pour over the tissue-thin sheets,
scratched from their binding, spread
beneath her knees. She whips screams

into the wind. Flails her windmill
wrists of blood for one
glance. One nod. One

raised brow from whatever forged
her bones then dumped her here—
boards beneath the bridge. Her voice

storms this shelter, desperate for one
set of hands to catch her.
First Chronicles, Second Chronicles.

She carves the gospels into her forearms,
and on her hands, her shins, mauls
the pavement for chunks of *Mark*.

She claws its text, convinced
that beneath the manuscript lies
a love letter penned for her.

From the smudges of chapter five
emerges a woman who'd been bleeding
for twelve years. Rabid, this woman

barges past the touts who've branded her
unclean, past the ones who've spurned her
for years because to them, she was

God's shitty draft. But she demands
more than a sentence. She claws past
a thousand callous sandals, then lands

at the right pair of ankles. Her face, forearms
to the desert. She fingers the robe
of the one man who sees no difference

between filthy and clean. He bends to her.
Calls her *daughter.* Beneath the bridge,
the girl's tear-torn lips shiver,

Where are you? Only a chill responds. A rat
yawns near a beer can.
As she lifts her hand to scratch again

at *Genesis,* a sparrow descends
on her palm. It patches her wounds
with its compassionate feet.

Mother Asks Whether I Have Ever Wanted to Kill Myself

The question, gentle,
startlingly unhesitant,

needles into the child
I keep cuffed to a cell

inside me.
                    I decide

not to lie. Then she
decides, also, not to lie.

She makes me promise,
I make her promise

and another sun
sinks into its Pacific bed

and another sun
elsewhere kicks awake

the flocks hymning
for the God who flickers
on my secular lips.

Every Hair on Your Head

Every hair on your head is counted.
You are worth hundreds of sparrows.
— Sparklehorse, "Hundreds of Sparrows"

The day you pushed a bullet through your heart,
the length of a day on earth shortened by a millionth of a second.

That same day, a NASA satellite captured an image of a dust storm,
Chile withstood its one hundred thirtieth aftershock in a week, and I
glimpsed a bird, twitching

on the floor of a Brooklyn metro station. Its eyeballs
bulged as if to literally absorb the ocular world,

and I shuddered away. For hours, I saw that flinching
creature in my mind. I saw hundreds of similar birds
shimmering into the station to lie

next to it—a quilt of silvery bodies tiled wing to wing. On good days,
I want to be saved. Most days, I want

every savior in our hell—so they'll know
torment in the bloodstream—death's whistling, ceaseless,
blurring the cleanest heartbeats.   My first time, I was thirteen.

I tested five pills. My stomach barely ached, I ate ramen, lived, solved
math problems. But for days before that, I envisioned my body
smeared. Inside out. A swarthy, dazzling canvas.

What I wouldn't give to graze that silence.

Did you do it standing up
or crouching?   Which was the bigger surprise—
                    the gun punching   or the angel catching you?

Angel Hunting

I swallowed Precious Moments drawings
for breakfast in high school. Bit inches off
eight by elevens with my molars,
my canines. Tongued the flat paper taste
of my father's pencil into wet crumbles
and swallowed—a cherubic boy, his teardrop eyes,
his handful of daisies, a cherubic,
teardrop-eyed girl with pencil-gray curls.

Then I tore into stacks of wide-ruled, sloppy cursive
confessions. I chewed, swallowed every syllable
my dad rambled from prison. I digested
each second, hour, week he cramped over those pages
to draw cartoon children with puffy farm clothes.

Who were those children? Did that boy grip his daisies
with my father's hand? Or was the boy a manmade
God with nothing to give but a sketched smile,
large God shoes that seemed to say
I could walk all over you. Or was it—*I could walk*
miles for you? A decade later, my father

still floods me with pleas. I wake up to an email inbox
choked with my father's name. One on top of the other
on top of the other like unshelved hymnbooks
humping each other for warmth in a church basement.

I don't look for God. God wedges God's way
into my veins without discretion. What I do

look for: the tiny angel chained
inside my father. The tiny angel who says,
Ask her for forgiveness. And the next day,
Ask her for forgiveness. And the day after,
Ask her. Ask her. Keep asking her. Whole years,
thousands upon thousands of days after he even remembers
the circumference of my mother's arms, my father still begs

for this. Forgiveness. I look for that tiny,

insistent angel in my father's teeth. I look for him
in the bump on my father's writing finger.
And on those nights I don't eat because I wonder
whether my father remembered to feed himself,
I almost find that tiny angel in those children,
still floating in my gut.

Sustenance

Jesus said, *Do not worry about your life,*
what you will eat or drink. Or about your body,

what you will wear. So you cleared
your cupboards. Lay naked on the shelf

where I found you. I mistook you
for a loaf I had prayed for. You let me

take you in my mouth, and I binged
on your flesh. Both of us—unaware—

we should have prayed for love
instead of crumbs.   Still now, small

morsels of you
                    on my tongue.

What Creatures Remain

Seventy species of wildly colored harlequin frogs—
gone. Also warblers,
wood thrush—songbirds whose ringtones
hardly startle. Tuned out
like my father's dialing, dying.

Father writes to describe his mouth, nose,
inflamed. Or was it, *in flames.* I ship
buckets of weeping to his studio. Just in case.

*

B's fractured skull. Swollen hunk of brain
sucking blood. Before the vodka bottle cracked him,
a barefoot man cloaked in a blanket
strolled past. Barefoot man said,
I'm walking with God.

Displaced in the west, B writes, *I expect the ocean
on my other side.* Unpacked
on the east coast, I know
that shock. Every mountainless morning, the sun
punches like a toxic fist.

*

Feeding tubes have infected
Grandpa's last lung. Bellicose cells fly everywhere
and Grandpa requests a leg massage.

Father writes, *Even in pieces,*
Grandpa wants to live. I suddenly think: how swiftly
the President flicks thirty thousand living, blinking
humans over the Atlantic.

*

What creatures remain endangered today?
What are their names? Do they die in clumps
because we've stopped calling for them?

In the storm, even the Empire State Building appears
ruined with bruises. I stand
on my rooftop. Absorb the downpour. An attempt
at surrender. —or prayer.

Selah

When the sky unhinges, how will we survive?

Who will extract the cancers
from our lips, the bombs from our arteries?

When we make delirious love
in the closets of our small, lovestarved God,
may he honor

our passion. Forgive
our poisons. May he unplug our churches—
fling every cracked bulb

back into the sky. And with each re-tinseled constellation, may he grow.
Like a hot organ. May he watch us come, come to understand

worship. That to worship is to survive is to be

wholly human, wholly
gripping the other hand.

IV. SPARROWS

—but now, I do not know why,
while the sky becomes clouded
and overcast with quarrels and curses,
a light rises on her side.

— Vincent van Gogh, in a letter to his
younger brother Theo, November 18, 1881

Between Heaven and the Bedroom

Somewhere in the city with her slip-proof
shoes and apron, our mom locates an angel
tall as miles. Mom pushes up her sleeves

and—at the angel's nod—sprints
to the back of the angel, grabs a fat sheaf
of wing—its feathers thick as ropes—

and climbs
                        and climbs. Every night

she climbs. And every night, she returns,
flakes of holy in her hair. She returns—work shirt
wet with angel drench—to a bedroom of crumbs,

half-eaten margarine and jam sandwiches
my small sisters and I assembled
on the carpet. She is grateful we ate something.

Then, her ear to our mouths, Mom listens
for sleep before launching her secret
lullaby—her sturdy hands on our foreheads—

her prayers pouring over us like torrents
of wild comets. And we are so entirely
awake—three little girls—good at pretending,

toughened from having to have been small adults
before Mom came home. Years later, the day
my sister's car spins across six freeway lanes

then stands, upright, unbent—my sister shaken
and unbruised—I discover a fleet
of little angels on their knees, cultivating

a humble garden in my bedroom. I realize then
that our mom must have come home
with armloads of them. She must have begged

for these little angels—collected them from God
like tip dollars. Or maybe they tumbled out
on their own—out of her infinite tongues—

as we found rest beneath her desperate whispers.

Sex Education

Folded into the carpet, eyes closed, I huddle
next to my small sisters—the baby
curled in the middle. My parents shuffle

in the couch bed beside us, and I wake. I peek.
I absorb the wet sounds of one mouth
guzzling another's laughter—and without

health class pamphlets, without Eve's Adam
and the fruit still rich on his chin, I learn

the music of bodies smacking together.
I learn the word *yes.* And how *yes*—

when whispered over and over—seems to free
other meanings—secret meanings

I never heard them speak in daylight.

Can These Bones Live?

Scripture says, *Lord, you alone know,* but with all my father's finger bones
moldy in my own, all I manage is, No.

You scatter my father's vertebrae in the dust and cover
my mouth. Yours opens: *Say to them, Dry bones, hear*

the word. You promise tendons and flesh. A cohort of dancing
bones, armed with your breath.

                                        But Sir, do you know my recent father—

his windowless home in Seoul I call "studio"
because people resist "tomb." During our reunion, he gripped me

at the market. Wept because he hadn't shopped with anyone
in a decade. He berated a man

near the tangerines. Tossed the oddest assortment of nuts,
dumplings into our cart. Every gesture

                                        frenetic. Lopsided. Too loud or too weepy.

At ninety-five pounds, I was allowed
one meal a day. No phone calls. I sat in one chair

for days at a time. His right eye twitched. He crouched
in the bathroom for hours sometimes.

When my father offered me a Vaseline-and-towel facial
because that's what he thought fathers do,

I yielded. I was twenty-two and I yielded
to everything. To say, yes,

that's what fathers do. Then one night, as he slept, I tore him open
to reorder his bones. I pressed

temporal bones to clavicles. Mandibles to hips. To fix him. I piled
wrong bone on top of wrong bone until I dissolved

into sobs, waking my father, who—like a father—
held the shell of my body

for hours. I heaved and heaved
into his growing shoulders, and he didn't ask why.

You say these bones can live, Lord,
as though you don't remember that in your story, one must die

for the other to live.
How many deaths have I to brave?

That first time I died, I wept tendons and flesh
into my father's rejected frame.

How long before his dancing bones?

Resolution

I curl into an ear
on bare hardwood. My bones
stay folded for days. They once
trembled at the slightest
buzz of the ethereal—

how have I since unlearned
how to listen?

How do I practice hearing
the sky?   —seizing the sky?

I want to hunt that ancient
language—that blood message
of banquets and cherubs
dangling from heaven like good fruit.
One day, the sky will open

like a mouth. It will pour forth
a thousand calling sparrows

and I will be ready.

I will answer every one.

Destination: Beautiful

I've come to hunt a time capsule at the west end
of Sunset Boulevard. To rummage the beach for remnants
of old friends who've abandoned each other to sprout

new families. Suddenly everyone has cleaved
to strangers made of diamonds and cake, capable of waving away
whole bruised childhoods—rotten fruits we used to feed

this drooling ocean. Years ago, a friend and I
hiked the Will Rogers trail. We caught a dim rainbow
at the cliff, where he stood and hid

his hands in his pockets. We sucked in the Pacific,
the traffic. We met an elderly man called Timothy—a retired
tour guide who slept in his car with a book of red-letter scripture

seatbelted next to him. I hoped I would die
on that mountain because I thought, *that close* to God,
it would be a hassle to send me to hell.

In the memory of that day, I am alone. The friend is there,
also alone. He leans from the cliff
and scans the city dots for his beautiful girl. His, now,

wife.   *Wife.* The word bends
like a soft branch in my mouth. I've learned not to choke on it
by lying achingly still. The waves reach and reach for me

over the black ocean. The tender, white hands of children petting a large, harmless corpse.

Psalm 107

Praise you for that blanket.

Praise you for the stranger
who draped it over my mother,

a naked girl perched,
pregnant, in the snow. Praise you
for my father

who said he'd kill her
if she ran. And for my mother,
who didn't run. Like a mannequin
or a stupid dog.

Praise you for her skin
the color of cold
jellyfish, her psalms
careening from her throat
to her belly, where your fingers—

praise your fingers—forged
my unformed body. Praise you
for my bloodline. For the savages
and the idiots, whom you love
the same. Thank you
for the bones you stacked in me

to brave this unsettling.

We Called It the Year of Birthing

God handed me a trash bag bloated with feathers. *Turn this*
into a bird, he said. He threw me a bowl of nails. *And make with this,*
a new father. God gave some people
whole birds. Readymade fathers with no loose bolts.
The rest of us received crude nests. Used mothers.

I banged the nails into two planks of wood
and marched around a church screaming, *Father, father*
until friends appeared, hammering
the scraps they were given to make something of themselves.

When beaten hard enough, some people scamper into corners
sordid with similar beaten people. Others of us—
the stubborn, unbreakable humans—weld our wounds
to form tools. Then we spend our days
mending bent humans or wiping the humans
mired by all the wrong fingerprints.

The morning the first baby was born in our circle of friends,
we hovered over this child who, unlike us,
was born whole. *You were given a good mother*, we said. *A good father.*
Each one of us prayed.   We scrubbed our soiled hands
before we held his swaddled body.

Testament

A small woman lives in a flowerpot in my closet.
She hates light. Brandishes her fists
                                        when she speaks. Not speaks—

mocks. She asks about my parents: *tell me a tragedy.*
I've practiced that tragedy.
But *this* is the truth:

I never feared him. I feared *her*—her radiance, her hymns.

My fear being   resistance to the impossible.
The impossible,   a woman who endured.

He never said one kind word to her.
My father, I mean. To my mother, I mean.

Where did she gather those   *You are beautiful*s
for my sisters and me?   How did she never empty of warmth?

The small woman in the flowerpot loathes
my mother's clean, clean bones.

She once dared me to spit in my mother's face.
                                                            (She didn't spit back.)

When I was fifteen,   my mother found me
in a bookstore with a boy   pressed against my body—his muscles,

his jaw. I *let* him mark me.
After years of raking her bruises
away from her daughters, *that* was the only night
my mother let me see her cry.

When God passed out mothers to all the beastly children
and wives to all the beasts,
how did he misplace my mother in that wrong pile?

And yet, her devastating joy.   That rosy voice
insisting, insisting   God *is* good.

Happy Couple

I approach your cross with a bouquet of eighth notes,
quarter notes—cold, black stems

clinking awkwardly. With one unnailed hand,
you take my gift. Shove it in your mouth

like a fistful of beansprouts. This is how you learn
your part. We harmonize. You scrape the sky

with that free arm. I shift my eyes
away. How I learn to cry. A hammer sits

quietly in my bag. Next to the last nail.
For now, we sing.

NOTES

"Pretty Universe": "Marion Avenue" refers to the intersection of Marion Avenue and Colorado Boulevard in Pasadena, California, where a church called Vision Christian Fellowship can be found.

"On the Anniversary of the War on Terror": First used by President George W. Bush in an address to Congress and the American people on September 20, 2001, the phrase "War on Terror" alludes to a military campaign initiated by the United States, the United Kingdom, and their allies after the September 11, 2001 attacks on the United States. By 2009, the name of the campaign evolved to "Overseas Contingency Operation," as preferred by President Barack Obama's administration.

"Contrition with Liquor": "Sunset Strip" refers to a 2.4 km stretch of Sunset Boulevard in West Hollywood, California. The strip is notorious for its nightlife.

"Deciding Not to Drown Today": The East River, a tidal strait in New York City, separates Long Island, including Brooklyn and Queens, from Manhattan and the Bronx.

"6,883 Miles from New York, My Father Is Alive": The distance between New York City and Seoul is roughly 6,883 miles.

"Every Hair on Your Head" is for Mark Linkous, who was an American musician most famously known for his band, Sparklehorse. This poem's title and epigraph come from his song, "Hundreds of Sparrows," which appears on the record, *Good Morning Spider* (Capitol Records, 1998). The epigraph echoes sentiments found in the gospel of Matthew, chapter 10, verses 30 and 31, and the gospel of Luke, chapter 12, verse 7. Mark Linkous took his own life on March 6, 2010. He pointed the gun at his heart.

"Angel Hunting": Precious Moments, Inc. is an American giftware company whose signature childlike, angelic figures were created by Samuel J. Butcher.

"Sustenance": The quote attributed to Jesus is borrowed from the gospel of Matthew, chapter 6, verse 25.

"*Selah*" is a Hebrew word, roughly translated to mean, *Let those with eyes, see; let those with ears, hear.* It is often used as a musical-liturgical notation in the psalms found in the Tanakh, the Bible, and the Zabur.

"*Can These Bones Live?*": The title and italicized lines quote from the story of The Valley of Dry Bones, found in chapter 37 of the Book of Ezekiel. According to the Abrahamic religions, Ezekiel was a Hebrew prophet born circa 622 BCE, and this story recounts one of his visions about the redemption of the exiled and the oppressed.

"Destination: Beautiful": This title is borrowed from the title of Mae's debut alternative rock album of the same name—*Destination: Beautiful*—released by Tooth & Nail Records in 2003.

"We Called It the Year of Birthing" is for Micah Rajan George and his unbreakable parents.

The cover photograph, taken by photographer Kathy Fernandez, captures a public art installation titled *Forgotten Songs*, found in Angel Place, an alleyway in Sydney, Australia. *Forgotten Songs* was created by artist Michael Thomas Hill to commemorate the songs of 50 birds once heard in central Sydney before European settlement displaced the birds from the city. Many thanks to both Kathy and Michael for their powerful artwork.

ACKNOWLEDGMENTS

Sincere gratitude to the editors of the following print and online publications in which these poems, sometimes in different versions, first appeared:

Berfrois, CALYX Journal, The Collagist, Connotation Press, elimae, Hyphen Magazine, Kartika Review, Lantern Review, Lo-Ball Magazine, The Los Angeles Review, Memoir (and), Mission at Tenth, Moonshot Magazine, Muzzle Magazine, North American Review, The November 3rd Club, PANK Magazine, Rattle, Relief Journal, The Same, Solstice Literary Magazine, The Sow's Ear Poetry Review, Tongue, and *The Wide Shore.*

"Every Hair on Your Head" was chosen by Claudia Emerson for inclusion in the *Best New Poets 2010* anthology (University of Virginia Press, 2010).

"Destination: Beautiful" was the recipient of the 2013 Neil Postman Award for Metaphor from *Rattle.*

I am indebted to Laure-Anne Bosselaar, without whom this book would not exist. *Merci beaucoup* for your generous spirit and thorough readings of many of these poems. This book is for you. "Because you will understand."

I am also grateful for the teachers and former students at Sarah Lawrence College for their guidance and support. Thanks especially to the following poets who made indelible impressions on several poems in this book: Victoria Lynne McCoy, Marie Howe, Cathy Park Hong, Thomas Lux, and to Kurt Brown, whose memory thrives in the communities he served.

Many thanks to Sarah Gambito, Joseph O. Legaspi, Oliver de la Paz, Vikas Menon, and the entire Kundiman poetry community for being the family that gives me "permission."

Thank you to the numerous friends whose liquor cabinets, futons, care packages, prayers, and relentless encouragement propelled my writing forward—especially the ones who have been on call from start to finish: Karissa Chen, Shannon Fernando, and Rini Rajan George.

Endless gratitude to Martha Rhodes, Ryan Murphy, Bridget Bell, and the Four Way Books team for nurturing this book into existence.

Love and hugs to my blood family—especially my grandparents. A million thanks to my sisters for being the best co-musketeers anyone could want. I love and admire you both. Thank you, Mr. H., for loving your wife. Dad, I love you. More than anyone can know. And I love you, Mom. You and your Spirit are all the proof I need.

In memory of my grandfather, J. J. C.

Eugenia Leigh is the recipient of awards and fellowships from *The Asian American Literary Review*, Kundiman, *Poets & Writers Magazine*, and *Rattle*. She earned her MFA from Sarah Lawrence College, and her poems and essays have appeared in numerous publications including *The Collagist*, *North American Review*, and the *Best New Poets 2010* anthology. Eugenia serves as poetry editor of *Kartika Review* and lives in New York City.